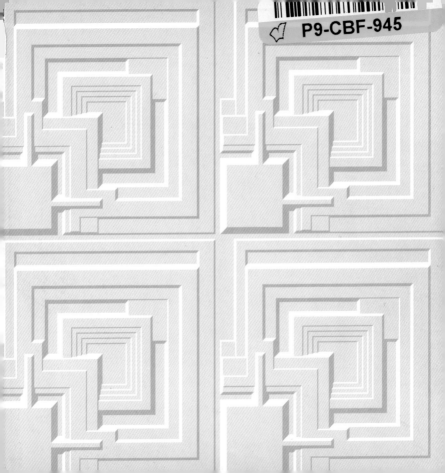

⠿ HUMAN BEINGS MUST GROUP, SIT OR RECLINE, CONFOUND THEM — AND THEY MUST DINE, BUT DINING IS MUCH EASIER TO MANAGE AND ALWAYS WAS A GREAT ARTISTIC OPPORTUNITY. ⠿

— FRANK LLOYD WRIGHT

AN AUTOBIOGRAPHY, 1932

FRANK LLOYD WRIGHT'S DINING ROOMS

▦   C A R L A   L I N D   ▦

AN ARCHETYPE PRESS BOOK

POMEGRANATE ARTBOOKS, SAN FRANCISCO

Library of Congress Cataloging-in-Publication Data

Lind, Carla.

Frank Lloyd Wright's dining rooms / Carla Lind.

    p.   cm.   — (Wright at a glance)

"An Archetype Press book."

Includes bibliographical references.

ISBN 0-87654-470-7

1. Wright, Frank Lloyd, 1867–1959 — Criticism and interpretation. 2. Dining rooms. 3. Dining room furniture. 4. Interior decoration. I. Title. II. Series: Lind, Carla. Wright at a glance.

NK2004.3.W75L56 1995   95-418

728'.37'092—dc20   CIP

Published by

Pomegranate Artbooks

Box 6099, Rohnert Park,

California 94927-6099

Catalogue no. A798

Produced by Archetype Press, Inc.

Washington, D.C.

Project Director: Diane Maddex

Editorial Assistants:

Gretchen Smith Mui, Kristi Flis,

and Christina Hamme

Art Director: Robert L. Wiser

10 9 8 7 6 5 4 3 2 1

Printed in Singapore

Opening photographs: Page 1:

Frank Lloyd Wright about 1930.

Page 2: The Lovness studio (1955),

Stillwater, Minnesota. Pages 6–7:

Dual seating areas in the Boynton

house (1908), Rochester, New York.

CONTENTS

URING FRANK LLOYD WRIGHT'S seventy-year career, many sociological changes affected the lifestyle of the American family. How Wright (1867–1959) adapted his designs in response to these cultural shifts can be seen most clearly in the evolution of his dining spaces. They record the transformation in cultural attitudes and economics that took place from the 1880s to the 1950s.

The separate dining room with special furniture did not appear in America until the eighteenth century. Before that, eating was done close to the source of heat and food preparation—often in the kitchen. As American society became more affluent in the nineteenth century, even middle-class families had some servants, but Mother still presided over the laborious tasks in the kitchen. Food preparation was separated from the serving area, and dining became more formal, with Father seated proudly at the head of the table. The turn-of-the-century home was where moral character was built, so great attention was given to its design. Despite Wright's desires to open the spaces within his houses, it did not happen overnight.

Wright's own homes mirrored his evolving ideas on dining rooms. Although his Oak Park dining space (1895) was enclosed, the family dining area at Taliesin in Spring Green, Wisconsin (1911–59) (opposite), was fitted into the living room—not set apart.

At the Robie house (1906), Chicago, the Prairie Style dining space is a distinct room. Its high-back chairs and table with integral lighting created a formal but intimate room within a room.

By the second decade of the twentieth century, mechanization and women's strides for equality began affecting family patterns. With Wright's help, the dining room began losing its walls and was transformed into part of the living space. By the 1930s eating had become less formal—moved back to the preparation area; for servantless families, the kitchen became the hub of the house. A comfortable, pleasing place for family and friends to gather for meals was important, but dining was a convenient extension of the preparation area, not separated from it.

These societal changes are illustrated by Wright's first two homes. His Home and Studio (1889, modified in 1895), Oak Park, Illinois, was built in the Victorian spirit, with a separate dining room—a special place of its own. But at Taliesin (1911–59), Spring Green, Wisconsin, the family dining area became part of the living room.

As early as 1896 Wright wanted to abandon the idea of a separate dining room and replace it with an assigned area in a larger space. But he continued to provide a designated dining room on his plans, probably because of his clients' wishes. He opened the space first to the

[The ideal dining room is a] bright, cozy, cheerful place you involuntarily enter with a smile, not larger than the necessities of this family and current guests required, perhaps a sunny alcove of the living room.
Frank Lloyd Wright
"Architect, Architecture, and the Client," 1896

Like most of Wright's later houses, the Usonian Exhibition house (1953), built on the site of the Guggenheim Museum in New York City, simply made the dining area the link between the kitchen and the living room.

garden and eventually to the living room. In a 1901 house design for the *Ladies' Home Journal,* Wright described the dining room as "coupled with the living room in that one leads naturally into the other without destroying the privacy of either." This plan places the living room, dining room, and library in line with each other, partially erasing the definition of each room.

Wright declared in 1908 that the primary functions of the main floor—reception, living, dining, and cooking—could be reduced to just one room, with "requirements otherwise sequestered from it or screened within it by means of architectural contrivances." As he sought to reduce the number of cubicles, he began to remove partitions separating remaining spaces. He used walls more like Japanese screens, suggesting movement rather than blocking it. Horizontal wood banding led the eye from room to room.

It was not until 1933 and the design for the Willey house in Minneapolis, however, that Wright actually joined the living, dining, and kitchen spaces—breaking down more walls to open up the American home.

THE DINING SPACE

PLANNING AND DESIGN

TO WRIGHT, THE REALITY OF A BUILDING was the space within—not its external form. Despite their redefinition, his dining areas grew from his and undoubtedly his clients' wish to make them featured spaces, suitable for the sacrament of the family meal.

Like Gustav Stickley, who encouraged a closer relationship with nature and called the dining room the "center of hospitality and good cheer," Wright respected nature. His early dining spaces reached into the natural world, often projecting beyond the rest of the house; rows of art glass windows were derived from plant forms, and he used murals of plants or flowers. In the Darwin Martin house (1904), Buffalo, New York, the room had windows on two sides and was in line with the pergola that led to the conservatory. The view from the dining table was usually the most beautiful in the house.

Most Wright houses built after 1936 had a dining area at the hinge point of the plans, adjoining the workspace (kitchen). Here, they often shared the masonry core on one side and the wall of windows on the other—a simpler, more open space but carefully articulated nonetheless.

⊞ The meanings of Wright buildings are made present in the experience of their spaces; the buildings do not "represent" some absent or displaced meanings, but engage the rituals of daily life ⊞

Robert McCarter
In *A Primer on Architectural Principles*, 1991

Changing in design several times over the years, the dining area at Taliesin remained in the same location. Top: Taliesin I, before the 1914 fire, and Taliesin II in the 1920s. Bottom: Taliesin III in 1925, after the second fire, and the space in 1940, similar to its appearance today.

FURNISHINGS

WRIGHT CAREFULLY CONTROLLED his dining spaces so that each piece was harmonious with the others. All the various elements—architectural features, built-in and freestanding furniture, glass, lighting, flooring, and wall finishes—were part of a total composition and shared the grammar of the building.

Along with other Arts and Crafts designers, such as William Morris, Charles Rennie Mackintosh, and Gustav Stickley, Wright produced furniture based on simple lines and a respect for the nature of the materials. He and his fellow designers were inspired by the theories of the day.

Wright began designing built-in cabinets as early as 1889 in his Oak Park home. Soon he moved on to the tables and chairs as well. Dining room furniture was easier than living room pieces to create and sell to his clients.

Wright's Prairie Style dining rooms are notable for their tall, straight-back chairs and large, heavy oak tables. This style persisted until the 1930s. While some of the later houses had tall chairs, most had lower backs, were smaller, and were built of plywood like the house. Each reflected its building's own geometric module and scale.

▦ Furniture is "built in" in complete harmony, nothing to arrange, nothing to disturb: room and furniture an "entity." ... All is so permanently organized, seeming to fit so well, we feel somehow that it is right that we should be there. ▦

Frank Lloyd Wright
"Architect, Architecture, and the Client," 1896

After Chicago's Midway Gardens (1913) went bankrupt, the furniture that Wright designed was never built. Wright's Midway chair no. 2 has since been produced by the Frank Lloyd Wright Foundation, along with a compatible table of circles and triangles.

The Goetsch-Winckler house
(1939), Okemos, Michigan,
was designed for two working
women. Like all the Usonian
houses that followed, its
dining space is located at the
junction of the kitchen and
the living area. The table
fits around the fireplace wall
like a piece in a puzzle. Its
modular seating, with upholstered chairs constructed of
plywood, resembles origami.

⌗ [E] very chair must eventually be designed for the building it is to be used in. ⌗
Frank Lloyd Wright
The Natural House, 1954

The simple plywood furniture for many of the Usonian houses was fabricated on site by the carpenters or in local cabinet shops. Some owners, like the Lovnesses, crafted their own furniture from Wright's designs. Their lakeside cottage (1955) in Minnesota uses a table and chairs that recall the dining set at the Hollyhock house.

⊞ The very chairs and tables, cabinets and even musical instruments, where practicable, are of the building itself, never fixtures upon it. ⊞

Frank Lloyd Wright
Ausgeführte Bauten und Entwürfe von Frank Lloyd Wright, 1910

WRIGHT COULD NOT HAVE CREATED his masterful dining spaces without talented and sympathetic assistants and artisans. Simply coordinating all the elements of so many simultaneous designs was a monumental task. But an artisan who met Wright's standards was certain to get a lot of work. One was John Ayers (1850–1914), a cabinetmaker who worked on the Bradley (1900), Hickox (1900), and other early Wright houses.

Perhaps the greatest contributor to Wright's interiors was George Niedecken (1878–1945) of Niedecken and Walbridge in Milwaukee. He began by doing renderings and murals but eventually coordinated many Prairie Style interiors, most notably the Robie (1906), Coonley (1907), May (1908), Irving (1909), Mueller (1909), Amberg (1909), Bogk (1916), and Allen (1917) commissions.

Among other cabinetmakers called on to do custom furniture for Wright houses were Matthews Brothers for the Darwin Martin house (1904); Barker Brothers for the Hollyhock furniture (1917); Gillen Woodworking for Fallingwater (1935); Harris Mill for the Zimmerman house (1950); and Leo Kelly for the Pappas house (1955).

Separate dining rooms

Wide openings to the living room, yet usually a separate dining space

Built-in features

Integrated cabinets and sideboards, usually with art glass doors. Bench seating in bay windows

Room within a room

Tall-back chairs and heavy tables, creating a room within a room

Oak furnishings

Quartersawn oak, red or white, with natural finishes and straight lines

Cozy nooks

Projecting bays, often polygonal with art glass windows

Multiple dining areas

Occasionally two spaces in a room, one smaller and informal, the other large and formal

Autumnal colors

A palette of natural hues: yellows, golds, ochres, reds, and greens

Human scale

Wood banding and light decks to define the horizontality, human scale, and flow of space

Fireplaces

A fireplace in the dining room or the masonry wall of an adjacent fireplace

Wood floors

Subtle geometric-motif carpets over hardwood floors

Simple upholstery

Plain fabrics with no pattern, such as velvets. Sometimes leather seats

Custom lighting

Special overhead lighting behind fret-sawn panels or glass. Lamps on the dining table, creating an intimate, protected setting within the larger space

Integrated fixtures

Radiators concealed with wood grilles to integrate the mechanical devices with the room's design

Open to nature

Garden settings visible through generous windows. Exterior plantings to bring the outside in

Natural art

Murals of nature to complement the natural views

Top: The Boynton house pantry (1908) and a Wright chair design for Midway Gardens (1913). **Bottom:** Art glass surrounding the Willits dining area (1901) and built-in lights at the May house (1908).

Elimination of the dining room

Dining areas, not rooms, to avoid wasted space

Combined dining-living areas

Center-house location, designed to share a masonry wall and a wall of windows

Adjacent to the workspace

Placed at the hinge point of the plan, often opposite the kitchen (now called the workspace)

Simplicity

Elimination of unnecessary items for the sake of efficiency, including separate furniture, bric-a-brac, individual light fixtures, radiators, trim, paint, and plaster

Built-in components

Tables and shelves often attached to the wall to conserve space. Dividers usable for storage

Flexible furnishings

Furniture pieces such as chairs usable in the living area

Modular systems

Components often built on site, using the same module, grammar, and materials as the building

Inexpensive materials

Usonian furniture usually built of the same material as the house, often plywood

Garden orientation

Overlooking the window wall on the private side of the house

Perforated wooden screens

Geometric patterns to filter light and create shadow designs

Indirect lighting

Concealed fixtures that reflect off the ceiling, some casting decorative patterns from beneath perforated shades

Warm colors

Cherokee red and soft golds the predominant tones, with yellow-greens and blues later

Simple textiles

Natural fibers and textures, often handwoven, with no patterns except natural weaves

Few accessories

Limited decorative objects such as weeds, branches, useful pots, and oriental artifacts

Top: The Rosenbaum house (1939) and a private dining alcove at Taliesin West (1937). Bottom: Garden view at the Pope-Leighey house (1939) and Japanese accents in the Palmer house (1952).

EARLY WORK

⊞ At no time do the members of a family exhibit a greater oneness of purpose than in sitting down together for a meal. In his early houses Wright consistently treats the occasion almost as if it were liturgical in nature. ⊞

Norris Kelly Smith
Frank Lloyd Wright: A Study in Architectural Content, 1966

The elegant Husser house (1899, demolished) in Chicago had Wright-designed furniture: a three-piece table with four light standards and twelve tall, slat-back chairs.

THE EXTERIORS OF MANY OF WRIGHT'S earliest houses, those built before 1900, looked fairly conventional, but the interiors began to show Wright's experimentation with space and details. The McArthur residence (1892) had a Wright-designed sideboard, as did the Heller house (1896), both in Chicago; the latter included designs for living room chairs and lighting, but no information exists about a dining table or chairs.

The first totally Wright-designed dining room was in his own Oak Park home, part of an 1895 remodeling. The polygonal china cabinet in the original dining area became part of the study. In the new dining space, the focus was on a large, quartersawn oak table with eight tall, straight, spindle-back chairs and a youth chair. The radiators were concealed, and the tile flooring continued up the fireplace wall. The carefully trimmed walls were divided into panels and covered with a gold painter's canvas. The lighting was recessed above a fret-sawn panel over rice paper. It was his first totally unified space, but it took him several more years to find a client willing to permit the same control.

Wright's Oak Park home, built in 1889 and modified in 1895, still showed a Victorian spirit. The dining room was separate from the living room, adjoining the pantry and kitchen. In his later homes, he removed the walls altogether. The child's chair was designed for his youngest son, Llewelyn.

P R A I R I E   S T Y L E

D R A W N   F R O M   T H E   M I D W E S T .   1 9 0 0 – 1 9 0 9

BY 1900 WRIGHT HAD FOCUSED HIS ideas of organic architecture into a design grammar that became known as the Prairie Style. The variations in his application of these principles were numerous: he created seventy-five stunning, harmonious dining rooms before 1913. The comprehensiveness of the design, including the number of special features such as carpets, intricate windows, and furniture, depended on the budgets and willingness of clients to give in to Wright's wishes.

Masterfully detailed and well-documented commissions were completed for Susan Dana (1902), Springfield, Illinois; the Darwin Martins (1904), Buffalo, New York; the Frederick Robies (1906), Chicago; and the Avery Coonleys (1907), Riverside, Illinois. Wright was also given great freedom in the Bradley house (1900), Kankakee, Illinois, and the Willits house (1901), Highland Park, Illinois. Historic photographs of the Fricke house dining room (1901) in Oak Park show a custom dining table but no chairs. The ceiling level changes over the table, with linear bands rising above to create a featured space. A smaller breakfast eating area was placed in the window

⊞ Wright's design, with its severely high-backed chairs and uncompromisingly formal air, had an ecclesiastical look, which was very much in harmony with the [Arts and Crafts] movement's emphasis upon the ceremonial, or ritualistic, aspect of breaking bread. ⊞

Meryle Secrest
Frank Lloyd Wright, 1992

In the Beachy house (1906), Oak Park, Illinois, doors opposite the fireplace wall extend the southern space onto a veranda and to the garden beyond. The smaller, more intimate tables were for family use or for after-dinner conversational groups.

· 31

bay, which received eastern morning light. Both looked out on a garden pavilion (since demolished).

The floor plan of the Henderson house (1901), Elmhurst, Illinois, illustrates one of Wright's earliest truly open dining areas. Like the Hickox house (1900) in Kankakee, the dining room and library were placed in polygonal bays of art glass on opposite ends of the living area. The Beachy house (1906) in Oak Park has a large dining room with separate alcoves. Its table, with lateral extensions, could be divided into three parts, two small ones for low-back chairs and a larger one for tall chairs.

The Boynton house (1908), Rochester, New York, has a larger dining room, with a southern garden exposure and two eating spaces; the ceiling height changes to mark the different experiences. Tables have lower light standards and additional light coming from art glass ceiling panels. The architecture and accompanying decorative arts gently embraced the diners with a sense of order and inclusion. The allure of Wright's dining rooms was in the sensations that these composed spaces elicited: warmth, happiness, safety, and delight.

At the Henderson house, Wright subtly articulated changes in use for the different areas of its grand dining space; overall spaciousness prevailed. The owners have used Stickley furniture from the period, as no Wright designs have been found.

⊞ Anyone who knows Craftsman furniture has no difficulty in perceiving that the principles upon which it is based are honesty and simplicity. ⊞

Gustav Stickley
Craftsman furniture
catalogue, 1910

32 •

The May house dining room (1908), Grand Rapids, Michigan (opposite), illustrates Wright's use of a massive table with attached light standards holding small planters. Every detail—tall-back chairs, custom carpet, art glass, floral mural, garden view, and wood banding—contributes to the feeling of repose and harmony that Wright sought.

At the Dana-Thomas house (1902), Springfield, Illinois (pages 36–37), the grand vaulted dining room has both a large table and a small one with shorter chairs. Autumnal murals and butterfly lights create a forest setting.

MIDCAREER ROOMS

FROM CALIFORNIA TO FALLINGWATER, 1917-35

The Hollyhock house (1917), which Wright designed for the unconventional Hollywood heiress Aline Barnsdall, had a discreet dining area next to the enclosed kitchen. Little residential furniture was designed in this period, but the Hollyhock house had its own, with ornament derived from the flower that became the house's namesake.

⊞ Miss Barnsdall had pre-named the house for the Hollyhock she loved . . . and called upon me to render her favorite flower as a feature of the Architecture, how I might. ⊞
Frank Lloyd Wright
An Autobiography, 1943

THE TWENTY YEARS FROM 1915 TO 1935 were marked by disorder, financial crisis, and transition in Wright's own life and rapidly changing economic and social conditions in America. The effects of World War I, the Depression, women's rights, the automobile, the International Style in architecture, and Wright's long tenure in Japan all made it a period of architectural reassessment. He continued to experiment, searching for new solutions. By the end of this period, Wright's career was reborn.

The final hours of the traditional dining room in Wright's residential designs seem to have begun in Los Angeles in the 1920s. Although his earlier attempts to eliminate the dining room combined it in some way with the living room, in the Millard and Storer textile-block residences of 1923 in Pasadena and Hollywood, the dining room is separated from the living room, placed on a different level and aligned with the kitchen. The Freeman house (1923), Los Angeles, provides no separate space to dine. A table placed near the window establishes the dining space. The informal, free-spirited lifestyle of Los Angeles of the 1920s called for original solutions.

At Fallingwater (1935), the celebrated country home for Liliane and Edgar J. Kaufmann in Mill Run, Pennsylvania, the dining area is near the fireplace and part of the large living area. The Wright table of walnut veneer is combined with imported three-legged chairs for better balance on the stone floors. Here, the Kaufmanns could entertain their weekend guests informally, in the arms of nature, without the pretenses of city life.

U S O N I A N   H O U S E S

R E S I D E N C E S   O F   M O D E S T   C O S T .   1 9 3 6 – 5 9

⠿ **He, in his architecture, sought to make the images of flow a fact, to celebrate continuous space and to bring all together into shapes which were unified by his will.** ⠿

Vincent Scully, Jr.

Frank Lloyd Wright, 1960

Lucille and Isadore Zimmerman's ceramics collection suited the garden-oriented dining space of their 1950 Usonian house in Manchester, New Hampshire. It even had custom-designed table linens.

BY 1936 WRIGHT HAD DEVELOPED a greatly simplified approach to residential design that he believed suited the contemporary American lifestyle. He called it Usonian, a word derived from his utopian vision for the United States of North America. His principal motivation was to create well-designed houses at a reasonable price so that middle-class families could have good housing. To do so, he employed machine technologies to cut costs and eliminated all that was not essential.

Each house was based on a geometric module, built on a grid incised into the red concrete floor. The dining areas—not rooms—were in the center of the house, opposite the workspace—no longer called the kitchen—and adjoined the living room, often called the garden room. Why waste space for an additional room, thought Wright, when overlapping uses could be accommodated?

Many of the dining furniture components were also flexible and could be used in the living room when needed. They were constructed of the same material as the house itself, usually plywood. The garden orientation of the Prairie years continued, as the living-dining area

was open to the window wall on the house's private side.

The unity and simplicity of the Usonian concept did not limit the possible design variations. As in all of Wright's earlier houses, elements were designed to be an integral part of the whole composition. The particular module chosen set the tone for the house. The triangular module of Mary and William Palmer's house (1950), Ann Arbor, Michigan, established the angle of the partial divider between the dining area and the workspace, from which the table extends.

For the L-shaped, board-and-batten house Wright designed for Sara and Melvyn Maxwell Smith (1946), Bloomfield Hills, Michigan, he used a rectangular unit. The dining table—freestanding, not attached to a wall as in many Usonians—is surrounded by squarely built chairs that reinforce the module. Perforated panels separate the space from the terrace beyond and can be opened on sunny days or closed for a cozier atmosphere. Their abstract patterns, repeated in the recessed lighting above, suggest the forms of stylized fir trees and create an embracing feeling of a pine grove.

Fretwork panels with elongated geometric shapes cast shadows like pine boughs on the table in the Smiths' Michigan home. The folded-panel-back chairs, grouped to form efficient benchlike seating, combine a triangle with the dominant rectangle.

It was generally agreed that the early kitchen units were too small. By the time the Rosenbaums built their addition, the kitchen had been expanded to include more room for storage and work space for more than one person.

Alvin Rosenbaum
Usonia: Frank Lloyd Wright's Design for America, 1993

⠿ Broadly stated then, the first and supreme principle of Japanese aesthetics consists in stringent simplification by elimination of the insignificant and a consequent emphasis on reality. ⠿
Frank Lloyd Wright
The Japanese Print, 1912

The open dining area in the Palmer house's living space is screened from the kitchen by a divider cabinet, not a wall. The triangular module establishes a dynamic, complex arrangement of angles within the simple but harmonious house. Japanese textiles, artwork, and a garden complete what Wright began.

PUBLIC DINING SPACES

MOST OF WRIGHT'S PUBLIC DINING ROOMS have been razed, leaving barely a trace of their details and furnishings. Gone are small works—River Forest Golf Club (1898), Illinois; medium—Lake Geneva Hotel (1911), Wisconsin; and Wright's most exotic and effusive designs for public dining—Midway Gardens (1913), Chicago, and the Imperial Hotel (1915), Tokyo. Only the Arizona Biltmore Hotel (1927) and the Riverview Restaurant (1953) at Taliesin, both collaborations, remain.

Wright worked for most of seven years on the Imperial Hotel commission to ensure that every detail was correct. The dining rooms were exuberant, with walls of lava stone carved into geometric patterns, colorful carpets and fabrics, hexagonal chairs echoing the low pitch of the roof, even china and silver service custom designed to enrich the dining experience.

Midway Gardens was Wright's design for an indoor-outdoor entertainment complex that combined the visual and performing arts with dancing and dining. Guests could dine outdoors or, in harsher weather, in the enclosed Winter Garden, a four-story feast of delights.

The Imperial Hotel's Peacock Room (opposite) and two-story dining room had their own china patterns. The colorful and tactile surfaces seemed to grow from the inner nature of their fiber.

In its vast Summer Garden focused on an orchestra shell, Midway Gardens (pages 50–51) welcomed more than seven hundred revelers. Wright-designed china and lamps mingled with store-bought tables and chairs—his planned furniture designs a victim of Midway's bankruptcy.

COMMERCIAL FURNITURE

⊞ Frank Lloyd Wright, the prophet of new ideas in architecture, now, for the first time applies his visionary ability to designing a group of dining room, bedroom and living room furniture. ⊞
Heritage-Henredon ad,
House Beautiful,
November 1955

The mahogany dining room pieces (opposite) included a rectangular extension table and sideboards. All cabinetry shared a carved molding in a dentil-like pattern. Upholstered tall-back chairs were used in the Rayward house (1955), New Canaan, Connecticut (pages 54–55).

IN 1955 WRIGHT CONTRACTED WITH the Heritage-Henredon Furniture Company to design a line of household furniture. It was introduced at the same time as fabrics and wallpapers he created for Schumacher. This was the first time that Wright designed for nonclients who could use furnishings in spaces not his own. While it seemed a departure from his philosophy of organic architecture—in which each element grows from the nature of the whole and is uniquely suited for that place—it was based on other fundamentals that Wright espoused. The pieces were geometric in form, celebrated the natural qualities of the materials, were solidly constructed, were modular, and were simple, with integral ornament.

Wright designed three separate lines, one based on the square, one on the triangle, and one on the circle. The seventy-five items that were finally produced were called the Taliesin Ensemble and incorporated elements of all three types, using the most conservative of the designs he submitted. While the furniture was of good quality, had a timeless, transitional appearance, and was considered a moderate success, it was not reissued.

Hanks, David A. *The Decorative Designs of Frank Lloyd Wright*. New York: Dutton, 1979.

Lind, Carla. *The Wright Style*. New York: Simon and Schuster, 1992.

Manson, Grant Carpenter. *Frank Lloyd Wright to 1910: The First Golden Age*. New York: Van Nostrand Reinhold, 1958.

Pfeiffer, Bruce Brooks, ed. *Frank Lloyd Wright: Collected Writings*. Vol. 1: 1894–1930. New York: Rizzoli, 1992.

———. *Frank Lloyd Wright Monographs*. 12 vols. Tokyo: ADA Edita, 1987–88.

Scully, Vincent, Jr. *Frank Lloyd Wright*. New York: Braziller, 1960.

Secrest, Meryle. *Frank Lloyd Wright*. New York: Knopf, 1992.

Smith, Norris Kelly. *Frank Lloyd Wright: A Study in Architectural Content*. Watkins Glen, N.Y.: American Life Foundation, 1979.

Wright, Gwendolyn. *Moralism and the Model Home*. Chicago: University of Chicago Press, 1980.

ACKNOWLEDGMENTS

The author wishes to thank Penny Fowler, Frank Lloyd Wright Foundation; Meg Klinkow, Frank Lloyd Wright Home and Studio Foundation Research Center; John Thorpe; John Tilton; Lynda Waggoner, Fallingwater; and especially the generous owners of the houses included here. Special appreciation is due Penny and Pat Fahey, Gabriella and Uwe Freese, and Mr. and Mrs. Milt Robinson for their assistance with new photography.

Illustration Sources:
© Peter Aaron/Esto: 54–55
Ping Amranand: 24 bottom left
Art Institute of Chicago: 10–11, 14 bottom left, 50–51
Gordon Beall: 28–29
Richard Bowditch: 8
© Judith Bromley: 23 bottom left, 30, 33; courtesy Dana-Thomas house: 36, 37
Currier Gallery of Art, Manchester, N.H., Bequest of Isadore J. and Lucille Zimmerman: 43
© The Frank Lloyd Wright Foundation, Frank Lloyd Wright Archives: 14 top right
Frank Lloyd Wright Home and Studio Foundation: 1, back jacket (H&S H 1042)
Pedro E. Guerrero: 13, 14 bottom right
Carol M. Highsmith: 24 top left
© Hillstrom Stock Photo: 49
Balthazar Korab: 18–19, 24 bottom right, 27, 44, 46–47
Christopher Little: 40–41
Paul Loven: 24 top right
© Norman McGrath: 2, 20
Phil Mrozinski, Frank Lloyd Wright Home and Studio Foundation: 29
Andy Olenick, Fotowerks: 6–7, 23 top left
© Judy A. Slagle: 17, 23 top right
Steelcase Inc., Grand Rapids, Mich.: 23 bottom right, 34–35
University of Kansas, Spencer Library: 52
University of Utah, Marriott Library, Special Collections: 14 top left
© Alex Vertikoff: 38

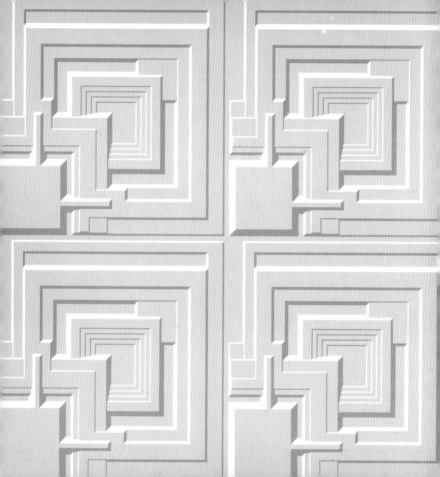